1990

THE LIFE OF
LAZARILLO de TORMES

THE LIFE OF

Lazarillo de Tormes

HIS FORTUNES AND ADVERSITIES

TRANSLATED FROM THE SPANISH
WITH NOTES AND INTRODUCTION
BY HARRIET DE ONÍS

BARRON'S EDUCATIONAL SERIES, INC.

WOODBURY, NEW YORK

*A translation of Lazarillo de Tormes by Harriet de
Onís.*

© 1959 by Barron's Educational Series, Inc.

All inquiries should be addressed to:
Barron's Educational Series, Inc.
113 Crossways Park Drive
Woodbury, New York 11797

PRINTED IN THE UNITED STATES OF AMERICA
9 10 11 **M** 3 2 1 0

PREFACE

Toward the close of the reign of the Emperor Charles V, at the moment of Spain's maximum power and prestige, there appeared in the year 1554 a little book, seven chapters in all, entitled *La vida de Lazarillo de Tormes y de sus fortunas y adversidades*. It was an anonymous work whose author has never been identified in spite of persistent scholarly research, although it has been attributed to various of the most important writers of the epoch.

The old adage "Great oaks from little acorns grow" could hardly be applied more appositely than to this brief work, which, in addition to its intrinsic value, carried in its blood stream the genes—to borrow a biological term— of many of the trends that were to characterize the modern novel. Its influence was wholly disproportionate to its size. Not only did it create a new literary genre, the picaresque novel, setting its stamp on all those of this type which fifty years later would begin to pour from the presses, first of Spain, and then of the rest of Europe; it also set the style for many of the modes that the new literary form—the novel—was to assume. The work was a mordant social satire, all the more telling for its apparent artlessness, and the device of its being seen through the eyes of an initially innocent boy. Its popularity was instantaneous and immense.

There are three known editions in the year of its publication, and variations in the text would indicate an earlier one which has not come to light. Even after it was put on the *Index Expurgatorium* in 1559 for its anti-clerical criticism, it continued to be published abroad and, surreptitiously, in Spain, where it reappeared in an expurgated version in 1573. It was read by all—learned and ignorant, laity and clergy—and was widely translated, ten editions of the work appearing in England alone between 1576 and 1672.

So deceptively simple is it in style and language, and the narration flows so naturally, that there have been those who believed it was what it purported to be—the autobiography of a *pícaro* or rogue, as the term was translated into English (in both languages the word was originally slang employed by vagabonds or "gentlemen of the road"), set down by himself at the request of a protector or patron. Fonger de Haan in *An Outline of the History of the* Novela Picaresca *in Spain* says: "My impression is that the author, whose name we can only hope some happy discovery may reveal, was a person who may have gone through precisely those adventures that he describes, being of humble birth and later of modest position . . ." This, however, is an assumption it would be difficult to substantiate, and most scholars disagree with it. It hardly seems plausible that *Lazarillo* could have come from the pen of a blind beggar's boy, who set out on his rolling-stone life at the age of ten, whose only school was that of experience, and whom we leave at the end of the book at what he calls "the zenith of all good fortune" as a town crier in Toledo. It would seem rather to be the work of a highly cultivated man, revealing on the part of its author a broad culture and exceptional literary gifts. His attitude in religious matters, and his criticism of human weaknesses and follies, would mark him as a man steeped not only in the ideas of certain philosophers of antiquity, particularly Lucian of Samosata, but very especially of Erasmus of Rotterdam, whose patron was the Emperor Charles V, and whose liberal, rationalist ideas had a powerful influence on Spanish thought of that period.

It was at about the time of *Lazarillo's* publication that the battle lines between Catholicism and Protestantism were being drawn up, with Spain, so many of whose outstanding writers and persons of prominence had been greatly attracted by certain aspects of Protestantism, finally championing the cause of Catholicism. Both a "hot" and a "cold" war were on, and if, as seems probable, the author was a man of standing, this may explain why he chose to remain anonymous. But for all his erudition and classical learning, of which there is abundant evidence, the author of *Lazarillo* knew how to give his narrative the quality of authenticity and verisimilitude, using the language its protagonist would have employed, that of the street and the market-place, the language which, as the poet Gonzalo de Berceo says, "a man uses to talk to his neighbor." This uninhibited, pithy style is one of the book's great charms. All the elements that would subsequently appear in the flood of picaresque or picaresque-inspired novels were already present in embryo in *Lazarillo*: the autobiographical form, the sly, terse humor, the unabashed honesty, not to say cynicism, the criticism of society, the didactic, moralizing intent. But the economy of form, the unity, the agility of narration that characterize the work, never allow it to become tiresome as is often the case with its successors. So entertained is the reader by Lazarillo's adventures and mishaps that only upon later reflection does he take in all the work's implications.

The novel is a literary form that has undergone a long process of evolution. There is a certain ambiguity in its very name. "Novella" was the term applied in Renaissance Italy to the tale or short story of the type made world-famous by Boccaccio and Bandello. "Romance" was used to describe a lengthy narration dealing with adventures of an extraordinary nature. The two concepts became fused in the modern novel. Congreve, the Restoration dramatist, puts the distinction nicely in the preface to his own novel, *Incognita:* "Romances are generally composed of the constant loves and invincible courages of Heroes, Heroines, Kings and Queens, Mortals of the First Rank, and so forth; where lofty Language, miraculous Contingencies and impossible Performances elevate and surprise the reader into a giddy delight, which leave him flat upon the ground . . . when he is well convinced that 'tis all a lie. Novels . . . come near us and represent to us intrigues in practice, delight us with accidents and odd events, but not such as are wholly unusual or unprecedented, such which not being so distant from our belief bring also the pleasure nearer to us."

During the late Middle Ages there had been an abundance of what, for the sake of convenience, we may call pre-novel forms. There was the "romance" of chivalry, so

well described above, which was the prose descendant
of the epic; its favorite themes were Charlemagne and
his exploits, King Arthur and his Knights of the Round
Table, and other heroes having even slighter links with
reality. There were the histories of two constant lovers
come down from classic tales such as those of Pyramus
and Thisbe, Dido and Aeneas; and the pastoral novel,
so popular in its day, inspired in the eclogues of Pindar
and Virgil. All these forms bore abundant fruit in Spain.

At about the same time as *Lazarillo de Tormes* there
appeared in Spain another brief novel, *El Abencerraje,*
anonymous too, which was also destined to have an influence on subsequent literature out of all proportion to
its size. Just as *Lazarillo* contained the seeds of the picaresque novels that followed it, and was a forerunner of
the eighteenth century didactic novel and of Realism and
Naturalism, so *El Abencerraje*—which recounts the valor
of the last descendant of one of the most noble Moorish
families of Granada, and his love for the beauteous Jarifa
—was the first of the Moorish, or Oriental novels, which
were so much in vogue during Romanticism and paved
the way for the historical novel. But both these works
lay fallow for a time, as far as their literary influence was
concerned, and it was not until fifty years later that other
and more elaborate works flowered from these roots.

To Spain belongs the distinction of having created the
modern novel with *Don Quixote,* the first part of which
was published in 1605. Not only was it a satire of the
romances of chivalry—and also, in a sense, the greatest
of them all—but it likewise subsumed most of the types

of novel which had preceded it, and blended them all into an unparalleled whole through the genius of its creator. After this meeting "at the summit" to produce one of the great classics of all times, the various tributaries diverged to follow their own course, some to sink into oblivion, others to become a swelling flood.

In a sense, the picaresque novel is the negation of the foregoing types. The protagonists of the pastoral novel were ideal beings, moving in an atmosphere of poetic beauty. The appeal of the Oriental novels lay in their exotic quality, their portrayal of an unfamiliar and—to Occidental readers—mysterious world. The heroes of the romances of chivalry were figures either imaginary or to whom time had lent a poetic aura, divesting them of reality. They were inspired by the loftiest aspirations, living by a code that admitted of nothing common or mean, whereas the picaresque novel dealt with sordid, unvarnished reality. The originality of this form consisted in the fact that it presented a new vision of life. In his endless wanderings the *picaro* brings us into contact with beings of the most varied sort. However vividly these other characters are portrayed, for all the realism with which they are made to live, their chief purpose is to represent the society of which they form a part, and which is under criticism. The *picaro* gives us his vision of society—society seen from the underside, the "worm's eye view" as it has been called.

The *picaro's* vision of society is, of necessity, partial and circumscribed. It is realistic, but focused on reality from a single angle. He sets out as a child or youth, poor and inexperienced, who must make his own way and look out for himself. He passes from master to master, from job to job, living by his wits. He quickly learns how little he can expect from his fellow man, and detects the shams and deceits and cruelty hidden under the most respectable façades. He begins his career in innocence and trust, and the disillusions he suffers engender in him a wariness of all with whom he comes in contact. But he has one priceless compensation for his precarious life: freedom. He is free to change masters, jobs, travel all roads, see the world. Aspiring to nothing but subsistence, he is free from responsibility. His life had something of the charm that the gypsy's or vagabond's existence holds for all those hemmed in by the walls of respectability.

In real life it was the growth of the cities and the influx of wealth into Spain that bred the *pícaro*. As Unamuno said, every Spaniard has a touch of the *pícaro* in him. He appeared at a moment when all Spain was on the move: soldiers to Italy and the Lowlands, Spain's European possessions; conquerors, government officials, and colonists to her American empire; students to the universities, both Spanish and foreign; members of religious orders travelling from convent to convent, all resembling the *pícaro* in their mobility and the ease with which they embarked on new enterprises.

Of necessity the *pícaro* existed on the fringe of society. As he acquired no trade or profession, partly because of lack of opportunity, partly because of his love of freedom and his unwillingness to submit to the restraints that a profession or steady work would lay upon him, he became a parasite who lived by attaching himself to anyone who would provide him with a livelihood, however meager. The background against which he was to be found was the city, in whose bustle and anonymity he could move freely, or the open road with its inns and chance encounters. In the country or in a small town, where everyone had his established place, the *pícaro* would have been an anomaly.

One of his favorite resorts was the city of Seville, that teeming port on the Guadalquivir, the gateway to the Indies, whose highways and hostels were thronged with the multitudes that flocked there, both nationals and foreigners, drawn by the lure of the riches pouring into Spain from America. And even though the *pícaro* received only the crumbs from this lavish table, still, as Lazarillo says, "The hard-hearted give more than the naked." Though he often fell into petty thievery and other acts of roguery, the *pícaro* was not, strictly speaking, a criminal; a vagabond, a vagrant with no visible means of support at times, but motivated by no desire to do harm.

For the purposes of fiction, this wandering existence he led gave the *pícaro* an unequalled opportunity to observe and reflect on the nature of society and his fellow man. His adventures brought him into contact with the most varied levels of society. Some of the masters he served were eminently respectable beings in the eyes of the world; but the *pícaro* saw them in their intimacy, and as has been observed, no man is a hero to his valet. The world at large saw these persons as they wished to be seen, according to the rôle they assumed, the disguise they adopted; the *pícaro* saw them as they really were, stripped of their outward trappings. The result is an indictment of society and its most honored members and institutions, and in the end the *pícaro*, for all his cynicism and abjectness, proves better—or no worse—than his superiors, from whom he learned his vices or by whom he was forced to acquire them in order to survive.

Fundamentally, the *pícaro* is the anti-hero, as Professor Chandler, the author of two excellent studies on the picaresque novel, has called him. All the attributes which had characterized the earlier heroes of fiction were lacking in the *pícaro*. Love, courage, and pride were ideals foreign to him. He is a marginal, negative being, and in his negativism would hardly seem suitable material for art. But he has the invaluable quality of being a lens through which we view society. And having foresworn all pretense regarding himself or his family, he is not taken in by the shams of others. One of the themes adumbrated in *Lazarillo*, where everything is implicit rather than explicit, which would be dwelt on at greater length in the picaresque novels that followed it, and which was to become a tenet of eighteenth-century thought, was that of man's original innocence—a foreshadowing of Rousseau's theory of the "noble savage"—and of society as the corrupting agent.

Among the outstanding achievements of *Lazarillo de Tormes* is that peculiarly Spanish gift for creating literary figures that take on a life of their own. Don Quixote and Don Juan are notable examples, and to these should be added one of Lazarillo's masters, the impecunious squire. Whenever one thinks of a proud poor man, sacrificing everything to his concept of honor and dignity, it is he who comes to mind. And the delicacy and depth of the relationship between master and servant is one of the finest strokes in this little masterpiece. Lazarillo's other masters, mean and avaricious though they were, at least kept him after a fashion; whereas it was he who had to maintain the squire, sharing with him the alms he begged in the streets of Toledo, or, when this was no longer possible, starving with him. Nevertheless, Lázaro loved and even admired him, and deplored their separation. This understanding and affection between two beings who represent completely opposed concepts and values anticipates the relationship between Don Quixote and Sancho Panza. Azorín, the great Spanish essayist, poignantly evokes in his book *Castilla* the last years of the squire, now wealthy, respectable, and ill, whose memory returns to the days of his youth in the company of his servant Lazarillo.

As has been previously pointed out, after a lapse of fifty years the picaresque novel became a favorite literary form, first in Spain and then in the rest of Europe. One of the earliest, and probably the best of those that followed *Lazarillo de Tormes* in Spain, was Mateo Alemán's *Guzmán de Alfarache* (1599). Subtitled "A Watchtower on Human Life," it carried to its ultimate conclusions the criticism of society initiated in *Lazarillo*. Its scene of action was incomparably broader, as its protagonist moved about from the various cities of Spain to those of Italy; its findings were equally damning and far more sombre. In Vélez de Guevara's *El diablo cojuelo* (1637) the stage is further enlarged. With the aid of his ally, "the limping devil," the protagonist is able to look through the house roofs and discover the secret life of beings at every social level, a life which is hidden even from their servants, when they are alone and off guard. It is the vision of the most searching "candid camera."

The influence of the Spanish picaresque novel on other literatures was very great. One of the French classics, *Gil Blas de Santillane*, by LeSage, is a direct imitation of this form, and was erroneously thought by some to be a translation. Bunyan, Defoe, Fielding, Smollett, and Sterne were well acquainted with the Spanish prototypes, most of which had been translated into English. (As earlier mentioned, ten editions of *Lazarillo* appeared in England between 1576 and 1672, and there were seven editions of *Guzmán de Alfarache* between 1622 and 1690.) When Fielding wrote on the title page of *Joseph Andrews* "Written in Imitation of the manner of Cervantes, Author of Don Quixote," he could with equal propriety have written on that of *Tom Jones* "In Imitation of the Manner of Mateo Alemán," even though, in keeping with the English tendency and his own unique gifts, it was character rather than teaching that was of paramount interest to him. Despite their often savage, corrosive humor, the Spanish picaresque novels were primarily moral tracts; whereas Fielding, for all his moralizing, was above all a humorist.

Two sequels to *Lazarillo de Tormes* were published, one in 1555 in Antwerp, anonymous like the first part. It is a work of fantastic nature in which Lazarillo, converted into a tuna fish, roams the sea; it is filled with allusions, evidently symbolic, whose meaning eludes us. In 1620 Juan de Luna, a Spaniard living in Paris, wrote another continuation of *Lazarillo*, which was published in Spanish and French. It has been comparatively unknown, except to scholars, although it is well written and gives a vivid picture of its times.

Neither of these sequels, nor any of its successors, could match *Lazarillo* in freshness and charm. The latter has an ease and an assurance that make it unique; it never belabors the points it wishes to make; and it conveys its teachings by indirection. Although at the time of its writing freedom of thought and conscience were menaced in Spain, they had not yet been stifled, and its author was able to attack the vices of the society of his day, and especially those of the clergy, without circumlocutions. In its clarity, its directness, even in a certain sunny quality it possesses in spite of its sombre conclusions, it bears the stamp of Renaissance art. Its successors tended toward the involved forms of the Baroque.

The same thing might be said of *Lazarillo* that Chesterton said of *Robinson Crusoe*—a direct descendant of the picaresque novels—to the effect that one of the most entertaining books in the world was written about how a man managed to keep from starving to death.

HARRIET DE ONÍS

FOREWORD

I consider it proper that happenings so remarkable and, perchance, never seen or heard of before, should be brought to the attention of many people, and not lie buried in the dust of oblivion; for it might be that someone reading of them would find something to entertain him, and those who did not delve too deeply would be delighted.

In this connection, Pliny[1] says that there is no book, however bad, that does not contain something good. It is especially true that tastes are not all alike, and what one man does not eat another craves; thus we see things scorned by some people and not by others. This leads us to the conclusion that nothing should be destroyed or discarded unless it is completely offensive, but rather should be brought to the knowledge of all, especially if it leads to no harm and may even bear some fruit. Were this not so, very few would write for a single reader, for it is a laborious task; and those who have undertaken it want to be rewarded, not with money, but by having their works seen and read, and—if there are grounds for it—praised. In this connection, Cicero[2] says, "Glory is the mother of the arts."

---

[1] *Pliny the Younger, Caius Plinius Secundus, 61-116 A.D. Eminent Roman tragedian and rhetorician. The quotation is from his* Epistolae.

[2] *Marcus Tullius Cicero, Roman orator, statesman, writer, 106-43 B.C. The quotation is from* Tusculararum Disputationem libro quinque ad Brutum.

Does anyone think that the first soldier up the scaling-ladder is the one who finds his life most distasteful? Certainly not; but the desire for praise leads him to expose himself to danger. The same is true of arts and letters. The theological student who is a candidate for his degree delivers a very good sermon, and indeed he hopes that souls may profit therefrom; but ask him if he is sorry when they say to him: "How marvelously Your Reverence preached!" A certain knight who jousted very poorly gave his coat of mail to the buffoon who praised him for having borne himself so bravely. What would he have done had this been true?

And so it goes. Since I confess that I am no holier than my neighbor, I shall not be sorry if this trifle, written in my graceless style, gives pleasure to all who share it and find it to their liking, and gives them an insight into the life of a man who has experienced so many vicissitudes, hazards, and misfortunes.

I beg Your Excellency to accept the humble handiwork of one who would have endowed it more richly had his abilities matched his desires. And since Your Excellency has written me for a full account of these matters, I thought it best not to start in the middle, but at the beginning. In this way the whole story of my life will be revealed, and those who have inherited noble estates may see how little is due to their own efforts, since Fortune favored them, but rather how much has been accomplished by those who have rowed hard and skillfully against the tide and reached safe harbor.

CHAPTER ONE

LÁZARO'S ACCOUNT OF HIS LIFE
AND PARENTAGE

Your Excellency, then, should know first of all that I am called Lázaro de Tormes, son of Thomé González y Antoña Pérez, natives of the Salamancan village of Tejares. My birth took place in the Tormes River, and from this circumstance I took my surname. It happened in this way. My father, God rest his soul, was in charge of a grist mill on the banks of that river, where he served as miller for more than fifteen years. And one night when my mother was in the mill, great with me, labor came upon her and she brought me forth there. So in truth I can say that I was born in the river.

When I was a child of eight they charged my father with bleeding the sacks of wheat people brought to be ground, for which reason he was arrested, and confessed, and denied not, and suffered persecution for righteousness' sake.[3] I trust to God that he is in Heaven, for the Gospel calls such people blessed. At this time an armada[4] was being prepared against the Moors, with which my father, who was out of town at the time because of the

---

[3] *John I, 20. "And he confessed and denied not; but confessed, I am not the Christ." An instance of the author's ironical attitude in religious matters.*

[4] Armada *was employed for military expeditions both by land or sea.*

aforementioned mishap, went as a groom to a gentleman who formed part of the expedition. And like a loyal servant, he laid down his life with his master.

My widowed mother, when she found herself without husband or protection, decided to seek the company of the good to become one of them,[5] so she came to the city, where she rented a cottage and prepared meals for various students;[6] she also washed the clothes of certain stablemen of the Knight Commander of the Magdalena,[7] and in this way came to frequent the stables.

She and a blackamoor, one of those who looked after the animals, became acquainted. At times he came to our house and left in the morning. On other occasions he came to the door by day on the pretext of buying eggs, and entered the house. When he first began coming I disliked him and was afraid of him because of his color and fierce expression; but when I observed that with his coming our food improved, I became very fond of him, for he never failed to bring bread, pieces of meat, and in winter wood to warm us.

What with the continuing visits and the conversations, my mother one day presented me with a pretty little pickaninny whom I dandled and helped to keep warm.

And I recall that once when my black stepfather was

---

[5] Note of irony. The proverb in question is: Associate with the good and you will become one of them.

[6] Salamanca was one of the four great medieval university centers, the others being Paris, Oxford, and Bologna.

[7] There existed in Salamanca at the time in the parish of the Magdalen a branch of the military order of Alcántara.

playing with the babe, as the child perceived that my
mother and I were white, and the other not, he ran
frightened to my mother, and pointing with his finger,
said: "Mother, the bogey-man!"

"Whoreson," answered the father, laughing.

And, though but a lad, I thought to myself when I
heard my little brother, "How many there must be in
the world who shun others because they do not see themselves!"

Our fortune so willed it that the conversations of
Zayde, as he was called, came to the ears of the overseer,
who, making investigation, discovered that he was steal-
ing a good half of the barley provided for the animals;
moreover, he kept pretending that bran, wood, curry-
combs, saddle-pads, and the blankets and covers of the
horses were lost. When there was nothing else, he unshod
the horses, and the proceeds of all this he brought to my
mother to raise my little brother. Let us not be surprised
that a priest or friar should steal, one from the poor, the
other from his convent, for their devoted ladies and to
help their own kind,[8] when love impelled a poor slave
to do a thing like this.

All I have told—and even more—was proved. For they
questioned me with threats, and like the child I was I
answered and revealed all I knew out of fear, even certain
horseshoes which, at my mother's behest, I had sold to a
blacksmith.

My poor stepfather was flogged and boiling oil was

---

[8] *Instance of the anti-clericalism typical of much of the writing of this period.*

poured over his wounds, and my mother was sentenced, in addition to the customary hundred lashes, never again to enter the house of the aforesaid Commander, nor to receive the ill-fated Zayde in hers.

Not to lose both bucket and chain, the poor soul gritted her teeth and obeyed the sentence. And to flee from danger and escape evil gossip she went to work as a servant with those who at that time owned the Solana inn. And there, suffering a thousand hardships, she managed to bring up my little brother until he was of an age to walk, and me to a good-sized boy who fetched wine and candles and ran such other errands as the lodgers sent me on.

At this time there came to lodge at the inn a blind man who, thinking I would make a good guide for him, asked my mother for me; she turned me over to him, telling him that I was the son of a good man who had died for the faith in the battle of Gelves,[9] and that she trusted to God I would not prove a worse man than my father. She implored him to treat me well and look after me, for I was an orphan.

He replied that he would so do, and that he was taking me not as a servant, but as a son. And so I began to serve and guide my new old master.

As we had been in Salamanca several days, and my

---

[9] *Battle of Los Gelves, 1510. Los Gelves was the name given by the Spaniards to the island of Djerba, off the coast of Africa. In 1510, after their capture of the city of Oran, the Spaniards sent an expedition of 15,000 men against the island. In a surprise attack over three thousand members of the expeditionary force were ambushed and killed by the Moors.*

master did not find his earnings to his liking, he decided to leave that place. When we were ready to depart, I went to see my mother and, both of us weeping, she gave me her blessing and said:

"Son, I know that I shall see you no more. Try to be good, and may God guide you. I have brought you up and given you a good master; look out for yourself."

And with this I joined my master, who was waiting for me.

We set out from Salamanca, and when we came to the bridge at whose entrance there is a stone animal that looks something like a bull,[10] the blind man ordered me to approach it. When I had done so, he said to me:

"Lázaro, put your ear to this bull and you will hear a great noise inside it."

In my simplicity I did as he bade me, thinking this was so. And when he felt that my head was against the stone, he lifted his hand and knocked my head so hard against the devilish bull that the pain of the goring lasted for more than three days. Then he said to me:

"Fool, that is so you will learn that the servant of a blind man must have sharper wits than the devil."

And he laughed heartily at the joke.

It seemed to me that at that moment I awoke from the innocence in which, as a child, I had been sleeping until then. I said to myself:

---

[10] *Bridge across the Tormes River in Salamanca. It is attributed to the Emperor Trajan, but he only repaired an earlier one which existed. At one of its entrances there is a prehistoric stone figure of an animal resembling a bull.*

"This fellow is right. I must open my eyes and be on guard, for I am alone in the world, and must learn to look out for myself."

We set out on our travels, and in a few days he had taught me thieves' slang. And as he saw that I was quick-witted, he was highly pleased and said:

"Silver and gold have I none;[11] but I can teach you much of the ways of the world."

And so it was, for, after God, it was he who gave me life, and though blind himself, lighted my way and trained me for the race of life.

I take pleasure in relating these childish things to Your Excellency to point out how much virtue there is in a low-born man's rising, and how much vice in the well-born who let themselves fall.

To come back to that blind master of mine and continue with his doings, Your Excellency should know that since God created the world, He never made a shrewder, wiser being. He was an eagle at his trade. He knew a hundred and more prayers by heart. He had a low, meas-ured, vibrant voice that made the church in which he prayed reecho, and a humble, devout, circumspect visage which he put on when praying, without rolling his eyes or twisting his mouth as others often do.

Besides this, he had a thousand other ways and means of extracting money. He claimed to know prayers for many and diverse purposes; for women who were barren,

---

[11] *Another ironical Biblical reference. Acts of the Apostles, III, 6: "Then Peter said, silver and gold have I none; but such as I have give I thee . . ."*

for those in labor, for those unhappily married to regain their husband's love. He foretold to those big with child whether they would bring forth a son or a daughter.

When it came to medicine, he boasted that Galen[12] himself did not know half as much as he about tooth-ache, fainting spells, and female complaints. In a word, nobody ever came to him with an illness that he did not immediately advise him:

"Do this, do that, pick out such an herb, take such a root."

As a result, everybody trailed after him, especially women, who believed everything he told them. Through the arts I have described he had good pickings from them, and earned more in a month than a hundred other blind men in a year.

But Your Excellency should also know that in spite of all he came by and had, never have I seen so close-fisted and miserly a man; he kept me starved, and did not give me half of what I needed. To tell you the truth, if I had not helped myself out with my cunning and wits, time and again I would have died of hunger. But for all his wisdom and foresight, I outwitted him so that always, or most of the time, I got the most and the best. To this end I played devilish tricks on him, some of which I shall relate, though I did not always come off unscathed.

He carried the bread and everything else in a canvas sack which he fastened at the mouth with an iron ring

---

[12] *Galen. Claudius Galenus, 130-200 A.D. Famous physician of antiquity. Not only eminent in medicine, but one of the most learned men of his day.*

and a padlock, and when he put things into it or took them out he did so with such caution and careful counting that nobody in the world would have been able to steal a crumb. I took the miserable portion that he served me, finishing it off in two gulps.

After he had locked it up, and was off his guard, thinking I was doing something else, through a seam in one side of it which I many times ripped and then sewed up again, I bled the miserly sack, helping myself not to bits of bread, but to good chunks of it, and bacon, and sausage. In this way I found occasion to make up for the devilish hunger I suffered at the hands of the mean old blind man.

All that I could filch or steal I carried in half-pennies; and when they asked him to pray and gave him pennies, as he was sightless, the giver had no more than made the motion of giving than I had the penny in my mouth, and the half-penny ready; for however quickly he held out his hand, the amount was already cut to half its true value by my exchange. The blind man complained to me, for he could tell at once by the touch that it was not a penny, and said:

"What the devil is this, that since you have been with me these women now give me nothing but half-pennies, and before it used to be pennies and often larger coins? You must be at the bottom of this."

Also he would cut short his praying and stop in the middle of a prayer, for he had instructed me that as soon as the person who had ordered him to pray was gone, I should tug at the corner of his cape. I would do so; and then he would begin calling out again:

"Who wants this or that prayer said?", as is the custom.

He used to set beside himself a jug of wine when we ate, and I swiftly took hold of it, gave it a couple of silent kisses, and put it back in its place. But this was of brief duration, for he noticed the shortage when he went to drink, and to protect his wine he never after that left the jug untended, but held on to it by the handle. But never was there a lodestone with my drawing power, for with a long rye straw that I kept for this purpose and inserted in the mouth of the jug, I sucked it empty. But as the rascal was so shrewd, he must have heard me, and from that time on he changed his tactics, setting the jug between his legs and covering it with his hands; in this way his wine was safe. But as I had acquired a taste for wine, my mouth watered for it. Since the straw trick no longer worked, I decided to make a little bung-hole in the bottom of the jug, and delicately cover it over with a thin wafer of wax. When it came time to eat, pretending I was cold, I would crawl between his legs to warm myself by the tiny fire we built; and when the heat of it had melted the small amount of wax, a trickle would begin to run into my mouth, which I put in such a position that never a drop was lost. When the old fellow went to drink, he found nothing there.

He was dumbfounded, cursed his luck and sent the

pitcher and the wine to the devil, unable to understand what could have happened.

"You can't say it was me who drank it, Uncle," said I, "for it hasn't left your hand."

By turning and feeling the jug, he finally found the opening and caught on to the trick; but he did not let on, as though he had not discovered it.

The next day, I was letting the jug leak into my mouth as usual without thought of the harm in wait for me, nor that the wicked blind man knew anything, and was seated in my usual position, receiving those sweet drippings with my face skyward and my eyes half-shut the better to savor the delightful nectar. The blind man felt that the moment had come to take his revenge on me, and raising that sweet and bitter jug with both his hands, he brought it down upon my mouth with all his strength, so that to poor Lázaro, who expected nothing of the sort, but on the contrary, as on other occasions, was carefree and joyful, it truly seemed that the heavens and all they held had fallen on him.

The affectionate little tap left me dazed and senseless, and the blow with the jug was so great that pieces of it cut right through my face in many places, and knocked out my front teeth, without which I have remained to this very day. From that moment I took a dislike to the cruel blind man, and although he treated me kindly and made a to-do over me and cared for my wounds, it was plain to see that he had taken pleasure from this cruel punishment. He washed with wine the cuts that he had inflicted with the jug, and said, smiling:

"What do you think of this, Lázaro? The very thing that brought on your illness cures you and restores your health," and other quips not at all to my liking.

When I was half recovered from my nasty punishment and bruises, thinking to myself that with a few more blows like that the cruel blind man would get rid of me for good, I decided to get rid of him; but I bided my time so I could do it with greater safety and effect. Although I tried to soften my heart, and forgive him for the blow with the jug, it was not possible with the abuse this evil blind man heaped upon me from then on, hurting me without any rhyme or reason, whacking me and yanking my hair. And if anyone asked him why he treated me so harshly, he immediately brought out the story of the jug, saying:

"You think this lad of mine is some innocent child? Well, listen to this and see if you think the devil himself could try such a trick."

Those who heard him crossed themselves, saying:

"So young and already so skilled in evil!"

And they laughed heartily at the trick, and said:

"Give it to him, give it to him, and God will reward you."

With this encouragement he did nothing else.

In return, I always led him along the worst paths on purpose, just to make him suffer; if there were stones, over them; if there was mud, through the deepest of it. And even if I did not go dry-shod, I was glad to lose one eye for the sake of plucking out two from him who had none. For this reason he continually held the crook of his staff against the back of my neck, which was always covered with bumps and skinned by his hands. And although I swore that I had not acted with evil intention, but because I could not find a better path, it did me no good nor did he put any trust in my words, so great was the cunning and wisdom of the scoundrel.

And that Your Excellency may see how penetrating was the wit of this crafty blind man, I shall relate one of the many instances that took place between us, which it seems to me clearly reveals his great astuteness. When we left Salamanca his idea was to go to the region of Toledo, because he said the people were richer, though not over-charitable. He backed up his decision with the proverb that says: "The hard-hearted give more than the naked." And we took the road that led through the richest villages. Where we found a welcome and good pickings, we stayed on; otherwise, on the third day we shook the dust of the place from our feet.

It so happened that as we were coming to a village named Almorox at the time of the vintage, a grape-picker gave him a bunch of grapes as alms. And as the baskets are roughly handled, and also because at that season the grapes were very ripe, the bunch was falling apart. If he put it in the sack it would spoil, and so would everything it touched. He decided we would have a feast, both because he could not carry them, as well as to put me in a good humor, for that day he had given me many cuffs and knee-thumps. We seated ourselves on a wall, and he said:

"Now, to show you how generous I am with you, we are going to eat this bunch of grapes share and share alike. We'll divide it in this way: you will take one and I one, on condition that you promise not to take more than one at a time. I'll do the same until we finish it off, and in this way there will be no deceit."

With this agreement we began; but at the second time around, the rascal broke his word and began to eat them two by two, assuming that I was doing the same. Seeing that he was not keeping his promise, I did not content myself with keeping apace of him, but outdistanced him: two by two, and three by three, and as many as I could eat at a time. When we had finished off the bunch, he sat for a time with the stem in his hand, and shaking his head, he said:

"Lázaro, you have deceived me. I would swear to Heaven that you have eaten the grapes three by three."

"I did not," I said. "But why do you suspect that?"

And the shrewd old man answered:

"Do you know how I know that you ate them three by three? Because I was eating them two by two and you said nothing."

I laughed to myself, and, boy though I was, I was impressed by the blind man's shrewd observation.

But not to be long-winded, I shall pass over many things, both amusing and noteworthy, that happened to me with this my first master, and proceed to relate how we parted, and with this conclude. We were in Escalona, the town of the Duke of that title, at an inn, and he gave me a piece of sausage to roast for him. When the sausage began to drip, and he had eaten the drippings, he took a coin out of his purse and told me to go to the tavern and buy wine with it. The devil put the idea into my head, and, as the saying goes, opportunity makes the thief.

Near the fire there was a turnip, long and thin, which not being fit for the pot, had been thrown there. And as at the moment there was nobody there but the two of us, and as my mouth was watering with the appetizing smell of the sausage, which I knew was all of it that I was going to get, without giving thought to what might happen to me and all fear set aside by my desire, while the blind man was getting the money out of his purse I snatched up the sausage and quickly put the aforesaid turnip on the spit. My master, after giving me the money for the wine, took hold of it and began turning it over the fire, trying to roast something that had escaped being cooked because of its defects.

I went for the wine, and on the way I quickly finished off the sausage. When I returned I found the blind old sinner with the turnip laid between two slices of bread, not having recognized it for what it was because he had not touched it with his hand. When he bit into the bread, thinking to sink his teeth into part of the sausage, he found only the cold turnip. He flew into a rage, and said:

"What is the meaning of this, Lazarillo?"

"Lacerated should be my name," I answered. "Are you trying to blame me for this? Haven't I just come from fetching the wine? Someone was here and played a joke on you."

"No, no," he replied, "the spit has not been out of my hand. That's not possible."

I swore up one side and down the other that I had had nothing to do with that transformation and change, but little good it did me, for there was nothing the shrewdness of that cursed blind man could not ferret out. He got up, grabbed me by the head, and began to sniff me. Like a good hound, he must have caught the scent of my breath, and the better to learn the truth, with the fury that possessed him he pried open my mouth with his hands to far beyond its normal size, and without thought stuck his nose into it. This was long and sharp and at that moment with his rage it had grown a handspan. The end of it touched my gullet.

This, and my great fear, and the brief lapse of time, which had not allowed the sausage to settle in my stomach, and above all, the wriggling of that monstrous nose which was almost choking me, all these things together were the cause of the deed and the dainty manifesting themselves and the owner's property being returned to him. Before the wicked blind man could get his snout out of my mouth, my stomach was so upset that it heaved up its spoils, so that his nose and the dark, half-chewed sausage emerged from my mouth at one and the same time.

God in Heaven, to have been buried at that moment, for I was already dead! Such was the fury of the wicked blind man that if the noise had not attracted people, I do not think I would have escaped with my life. They dragged me out of his hands, which were filled with the few hairs left on my head. My face was scratched, and my neck and throat were gashed. The latter well deserved this, for its sins had brought me so much punishment.

The old devil told all who had gathered around us of my villainies, and repeated over and again the business of the wine jug and the bunch of grapes and what had just taken place. The laughter was so uproarious that everyone passing by the street came in to see what was going on; and the blind man related my deeds with so much wit and grace that, suffering and weeping as I was, it seemed to me I did him an injustice by not laughing, too.

Afterwards it occurred to me how cowardly and careless I had been, and I cursed myself for it, in not leaving him noseless, for I had such a good opportunity when the job was half done. I had only to clench down my teeth and there it would have been, and being that scoundrel's, perhaps my stomach would have kept it down better than it did the sausage, and when it did not show up, I could have denied the accusation. Would to God I had done it, for it would have been a good idea.

The hostess of the inn and those who had gathered around finally made peace between us, and with the wine I had brought to drink they washed my face and throat. About this the wicked blind man went on making jests, saying:

"Verily, I lay out more wine on this lad's ablutions in one year than I drink in two. The fact is, Lázaro, that you are more in debt to wine than to your father, for he engendered you once, while wine has given you life a thousand times."

And then he went on to relate how many times he had cracked my pate and furrowed my face, and then cured me with wine.

"I'm telling you," he said, "that if anyone in this world is to be blessed with wine, it will be you."

Those who were washing me laughed heartily at this, though I protested. But the forecast of the blind man was not wrong, and many times since I have remembered that man, who must have had the gift of prophecy, and I regret the troubles I caused him. I repaid him well, however, considering that what he told me that day turned out to be so true, as your Excellency shall hear.

In view of this and the wicked jokes the blind man played on me, I had decided once and for all to leave him; and as I had been thinking about it and planning it, with this last trick he played on me my mind was made up all the more. It so happened that the next day we set out to ask alms through the town. It had rained hard the night before, and as it was still raining that day, he was saying his prayers under the arcades in the town so we would not get wet. But as night was coming on and the rain did not let up, he said to me:

"Lázaro, this is a stubborn rain, and it's going to get heavier with nightfall. Let's get back to the inn in time."

To get there we had to cross a brook which the rain had greatly swollen.

I said to him: "Uncle, the brook is very wide now; but, if you like, I see a place where we can cross more quickly without getting wet, for it narrows there and with a jump we can cross dryshod."

The advice seemed good to him, and he said:

"You're a clever lad, and for that reason I like you. Lead me to the place where the brook narrows, for it is winter and water does one harm, especially getting the feet wet."

When I saw how my plan was working out, I led him from under the arcade and straight toward a pillar or post of stone, which stood in the square, and upon which and others like it, the eaves of those houses rested. I said to him:

"Uncle, here is the narrowest crossing of the brook."

As it was raining hard and the old fellow was getting wet, in his anxiety to get out of the rain that was drenching us, and above all, because God on that occasion blinded his understanding, so I could avenge myself on him, he trusted me and said:

"Put me in front of it, and you jump over the brook."

I brought him squarely in front of the pillar, gave a jump and got behind the post; and like a person awaiting the rush of a bull, I said to him:

"Come on! Give a big jump so you will land on this side of the water."

The words were not out of my mouth when the poor old fellow charged like a goat, taking a step back to get a running start and leap farther. He jumped with all his strength, landing headfirst against the pillar, which echoed as though it had been hit with a big squash; then he fell backward, half dead and with his head split open.

"How was it you could smell the sausage and not the post? Smell it! Smell it!," I said to him, and left him in the hands of the crowd that had gathered around him. I reached the gate of the city at a good trot, and before nightfall I was in Torrijos. I never knew what God did with him, nor did I take the trouble to find out.

CHAPTER TWO

HOW LÁZARO ENTERED THE SERVICE
OF A PRIEST AND THE THINGS
THAT HAPPENED TO HIM

The next day, not feeling myself safe there, I went on to a village known as Maqueda where, for my sins, I encountered a priest who, when I asked him for alms, inquired if I knew how to assist at Mass. I told him I did, which was the truth. For in spite of his ill usage, that sinner of a blind man taught me a thousand good things, and this was one of them. In the end the priest engaged me.

I fell out of the frying pan and into the fire. For, compared with this master, the blind man was an Alexander the Great,[13] in spite of his being, as I have said, miserliness personified. I can only say that all the stinginess in the world was housed in this new one. I do not know if he was born that way, or had acquired it with his clerical garb.

He had an old chest which he kept locked with a key that he carried tied to his cassock. When the holy bread was brought from the church it was immediately deposited in the chest, which was then locked again. In the whole house there was not a morsel of food as is to be found in others: a flitch of bacon hanging in the chim-

---

[13] *Alexander the Great was a symbol of munificence, generosity.*

neyplace, a cheese on a shelf or in the cupboard, a basket
with pieces of bread left over from the meal. It seems to
me that even if I had not eaten them, the mere sight of
them would have comforted me.

There was only a string of onions behind the locked
door of a room in the attic. Of these I was apportioned
one every four days, and when I asked for the key to go
for it, if anyone was around, he would reach for a purse
he carried in his bosom, carefully remove the key, and
give it to me, saying:

"Take it and have your dainties, and then give it back
to me."

As if all the sweetmeats of Valencia were there, when,
as I said, there was nothing in the aforesaid room but the
onions hanging from a nail! Of these, too, he kept careful
count, and if, for my sins, I took more than my ration I
paid dearly for it.

In a word, I was dying of hunger. But though he
showed me so little charity, he was kinder to himself.
Five pennyworth of meat was his daily outlay for dinner
and supper. To be sure, he shared the broth with me,
but devil a bite of the meat came my way: only a little
bread, and would to God it had been the half of what I
needed.

In this part of the country on Saturdays they eat lamb's
head, and he would send me for one, the price of which
was three *maravedís*. He cooked it and ate the eyes and
the tongue and the neck and the brains and the jowl
meat, and gave me the bare bones. And he served them
to me on a plate, saying:

"Take this, eat, celebrate, for the world is yours. You live a better life than the Pope."

"May God give you the same," said I to myself.

After three weeks with him, I had become so thin that I could not stand on my legs from pure hunger. I saw clearly that I was bound for the grave if God or my wits did not help me. There was no opportunity for me to employ my arts, for there was nothing to steal. And even if there had been, I could not deceive him as I did the other. (May God forgive him if he died of that blow on the head.) For with all his astuteness, as he lacked that most valuable of senses, he could not see me; whereas no one had as keen sight as this one.

When we reached the offertory, never a penny dropped into the collection plate that he did not take note of. One eye was on the congregation and the other on my hands. His eyes rolled in their sockets as though they were quicksilver. He kept account of every penny that was contributed. And the minute the offertory was ended, he took the plate from me and put it on the altar.

I was not able to relieve him of one penny during all the time I lived, or rather, died with him. I never brought him a pennyworth of wine from the tavern, for the little that went into the chest from the offerings he rationed so that it lasted him all week.

And to cover up his miserliness he said to me:

"Now see, boy, priests must be very temperate in their eating and drinking, and for that reason I do not go around begging like others."

But the wretch lied, for at religious gatherings and

wakes where we prayed, he ate like a wolf and drank more than a leech at others' expense.

And speaking of wakes, God forgive me, but I was never an enemy of mankind except then. And this was because on such occasions we ate well and I stuffed myself. I hoped and even prayed to God that each day someone would die. And when we administered the sacraments to the sick, especially the last rites, as the priest ordered all present to pray, I was not remiss in this, and with all my heart and will I prayed the Lord not that His will be done, as the phrase goes, but to carry the patient off from this world.

When one of them was saved, God forgive me, I sent him to the devil a thousand times; and the one who died received an equal number of blessings from me. For in all the time I was there, which was about six months, only twenty persons died, and I do believe that I killed them or, to put it better, they died at my request; because the Lord, taking account of my desperate, unending death, was pleased to kill them to give me life. But for my daily sufferings I found no cure, for if on the day we buried them I lived, the days on which there were no dead, after knowing what it was to be full, my customary hunger was harder to bear. So I found relief in nothing except in death, which at times I desired as much for myself as for others; but I never beheld it, though it was always in me.

I thought many times of leaving that miserly master, but gave it up for two reasons. First, because I could not depend on my legs, which were so weak from sheer hunger; and second, because turning it over in my mind, I said to myself:

"I have had two masters; with the first I was starved to death, and when I left him I encountered this one who has me on the brink of the grave; if I forswear this one and find another who is worse, what is left me but to perish?"

As a result, I did not venture to make a move, because I firmly believed that every change would be for the worse. And if I went one step lower no one would ever hear of Lázaro again in this world.

In this state of tribulation (may God save all faithful Christians from such), and without knowing which way to turn, seeing that I was going from bad to worse, one day when my miserly wretch of a master was out of town, a tinker happened to call at the door, who I do believe was an angel sent by the hand of God in that guise. He asked me if there was anything to be mended.

"You would have plenty to do on me, and it would be no small job if you could repair me," I said under my breath so he could not hear.

But this was not the occasion to waste time jesting, so inspired by the Holy Ghost, I said to him:

"Uncle, I have lost the key to this chest and I am afraid my master will beat me. Be good enough to see if among those you have there is one that fits, and I will pay you."

That angelic tinker began to try first one and then another of those on the big ring he carried, and I helped him with my feeble prayers. Before I knew it, I saw the face of God in the form of loaves of bread within the chest. When it was open I said to him:

"I have no money to give you for the key, but take your pay out of that."

And he took one of the loaves, the one he thought best, and giving me the key he departed happy, leaving me more so. But I did not touch anything for the moment, so the loss would not be noted, and also because when I saw myself the master of such great riches, it seemed to me that my hunger was appeased. When my miser of a master arrived, God so willed it that he did not notice the loaf the angel had carried away.

The next day when he left the house I opened my breadly paradise, and taking a loaf between my hands and teeth, in the time it takes to say two creeds I made it invisible; and I did not forget to lock the chest. I began to sweep the house joyously, for it seemed to me that with that remedy my miserable life would henceforth be improved. And in this way I was happy that day and the next. But it was not my fortune that this relief should last long, for on the third the tertian[14] laid me low.

For when I least expected it I saw the one who was killing me of hunger bent over our chest, rummaging around in it, counting and recounting the bread. I hid my concern, and repeating to myself prayers and supplications, said:

"Saint John, strike him blind!"

---

[14] *A species of malaria in which the fever returns every third day. There is a play on words in "third" and "tertian."*

After he had been making the count for a long time, by days and on his fingers, he said:

"If I did not keep this chest so carefully guarded, I would say that loaves of bread had been taken from it; but from today on, to close the door against this suspicion, I shall keep careful account of them. There are nine, and a piece."

"May God send you nine plagues," I said to myself.

It seemed to me that his words had gone through my heart like a hunter's arrow, and hunger began to rowel my stomach at the thought of returning to the past diet. He left the house, and I, to console myself, opened the chest, and when I saw the bread I began to adore it without venturing to receive it.[15] I counted the loaves to see if by chance the wretch had made a mistake, and I found his count righter than I would have wished. The most I could do was to implant a thousand kisses on them, and as delicately as I could, remove from the broken one a bit of the cut surface, and that had to do me for that day, less happy than the previous one.

But as my hunger grew, especially as my stomach had become accustomed to more bread during the two or three aforesaid days, I was dying an evil death, and all I did when I was alone was to open and close the chest and gaze upon that face of God, as the children say. But that same God who succors the afflicted, seeing me in such extremity, brought to my mind a palliative. For, considering things, I said:

"This chest is big and old and cracked in spots, though

---

[15] *Ironical allusion to the Holy Communion.*

the holes are small. It might be thought that mice had got into it, and nibbled the bread. It would not be good to take a whole loaf, because its lack would be noted by him who makes me live lacking so much. But this can easily be endured."

And I began to crumble the bread upon some not too costly cloths that were there, and I took this one and left that one, so that from each of three or four I crumbled a little. Then as one takes candy, I ate it, and comforted myself somewhat. But when he came for dinner and opened the chest, he saw the harm that had been done, and undoubtedly thought it the work of mice. For it was well imitated, in the way that they do it. He examined the chest from one end to the other, and found certain holes by which he suspected that they had entered. He called me, saying:

"Lázaro, look; look at the damage our bread suffered last night."

And I pretended to be amazed, asking him what it could be.

"What could it be!" he answered. "Mice, which leave nothing alone."

We sat down to eat, and God so willed it that even in this matter things went well with me. More bread came my way than the miserable portion he usually gave me. For he sliced off with a knife all that he thought the mice had been at, saying:

"Here, eat this, for the mouse is a clean animal."

And so that day, my ration increased by the work of my hands (or my nails, to be more exact), after we had finished eating, even though for me it never began.

Later I suffered another fright, when I saw him busily removing nails from the walls and seeking out boards with which he nailed and closed all the holes in the old chest.

"Oh, my Lord," I said, "how much suffering, misfortune and disaster must we mortals undergo, and how fleeting are the pleasures of our weary life! Here I was expecting this sorry remedy to relieve my poverty and make it endurable, and I was even somewhat happy and confident. But my ill fortune willed otherwise, arousing this miser of my master, and making him more diligent than he already was by nature (for this is a quality misers rarely lack); now, in closing the holes of the chest, he is locking the door of my consolation and opening it to my misfortunes."

Thus I was lamenting while my industrious carpenter concluded his labors with many nails and boards, saying:

"Now sirs, you rascally rodents, you had better change your plans, for you will not prosper in this house."

As soon as he had left the house, I went to examine his work and found that he had not left in the poor old chest an opening through which even a mosquito could enter. I opened it with my useless key, despairing of profiting thereby, and saw the two or three loaves of bread which my master thought the mice had got at, and I managed to pinch a bit from them, touching them lightly, like a skilled fencer. As necessity is the best teacher, and since mine was always so great, I thought day and night about what I could do to keep myself alive. And I believe that in finding these wretched remedies I was guided by the light of hunger, for they say it sharpens the wits, whereas satiety does the contrary, and this is certainly what happened with me.

Unable to sleep one night for thinking of this, and wondering in what way I could manage to outwit the chest, I noticed that my master was sound asleep, as his customary snoring and snorts revealed. I got up very quietly. During the day I had been thinking about what to do, and had left an old knife lying about where I could find it. I approached the dilapidated chest, and where I had observed that its defenses were weakest, I attacked it with the knife, which I used as a kind of auger. And as the ancient chest, weighted down by its years, lacked strength and valor, but was instead soft and rotted, it surrendered to me at once, and admitted of a good-sized breach in its side for my benefit. Once this was accomplished, I noiselessly opened the wounded chest, and feeling around for the broken bread, I did with it what I have previously told. Somewhat stayed with this, I locked it again, and returned to my straw, on which I rested and slept a little, but badly, which I attributed to not eating. And this must have been the reason, for at that age the cares of the king of France should not have robbed me of my sleep.

The next day the damage was noted by my master, both to the bread and the hole that I had made, and he began to curse the mice and say:

"Now what shall we say to this? We have never been troubled with mice in this house up to now!"

And without doubt he was telling the truth. For if there was a house in the whole kingdom they would have spared, it was that one, and with good reason, for they are not in the habit of living where there is nothing to eat. Once more he searched the house and walls for nails and boards, and mended the hole. As soon as night had come with its repose, I was up and at my labors; and as many holes as he stopped up by day I unstopped by night.

Thus it went, and we followed so closely on one another's heels that the old saying was very appropriate here: "If one door closes, another opens." In a word, it seemed that we were each at work on Penelope's cloth,[16] for what he wove during the day I ripped out at night. In a few days and nights we had left our poor larder in such shape that it looked more like an old battered breastplate than a chest, with all the nails and tacks in it.

When he saw his measures were of no avail, he said:

"This chest is so worn, and the wood so old and flimsy, that ne'er a mouse can it withstand. And it is in such a state that if we do any more to it, it will leave us completely unprotected. Bad as it is, and though it does little, once it is gone it will be missed, and will put me to the outlay of three or four *reales*. The best remedy I can think of, as that used up to now has proved fruitless, is to set a trap inside it for these cursed mice."

---

[16] *Penelope, wife of Ulysses, promised the suitors who importuned her to remarry, in view of Ulysses' delay in returning home, that she would make her choice when she had completed a shroud she was weaving. What she wove by day she ripped out at night.*

Then he went out and borrowed a mouse trap, and with cheese parings which he begged from the neighbors, the trap was kept set inside the chest. This was a big help to me, for in view of the fact that I did not need sauces to whet my appetite, I found pleasure in the cheese parings I removed from the trap; but I did not neglect my mousings of the loaves.

When he found the bread nibbled and cheese gone without catching the mouse that ate it, he was furious, and asked the neighbors what it could be that ate the cheese, removing it from the trap without being caught and the trap sprung?

The neighbors decided it was not a mouse that was doing the damage, for sooner or later it would have been caught. One neighbor said:

"I recall that there used to be a snake around your house, and that is undoubtedly what it is. It must be that; for as it is long, it can take the bait, and even though the trap goes off, as it has not gone all the way in, it can get out again."

All those who heard him agreed, and my master was greatly upset, and from then on he did not sleep so soundly. Any borer that he heard by night in the wood, he thought was the snake gnawing the chest. Right away he was up on his feet with a club that he kept at the head of his bed ever since they had told him about the snake, and he delivered mighty blows against the poor chest, thinking to frighten it away. He awoke the neighbors with the noise he made, and kept me from sleeping. He would come to my straw and stir it around, and me with it, thinking it might have come where I was and got into my straw or into my jacket, because they had told him that at night it often happened that these animals, seeking warmth, would get into babies' cradles and even bite them and do them harm.

Most of the times I pretended to be asleep, and in the morning he would say to me:

"Boy, didn't you hear anything last night? I was after the snake, and I think it might even go to your bed, for they are very cold-blooded and like warmth."

"Please God it doesn't bite me," I said. "I'm very much afraid of them."

With all this, I was so disturbed and wakeful that the so-called "snake" was afraid to go near the chest at night or do any nibbling; but during the day while he was at church or about the village, I made my raids. When he saw the damage and the impossibility of putting a stop to it, he prowled about at night, as I have described, like an uneasy spirit.

I was afraid that with all that vigilance he might discover the key which I kept hidden under the straw, and it seemed to me safer to put it in my mouth at night. Because ever since I had been with the blind man I had so often used it as a pouch that I could keep up to twelve or fifteen *maravedís* in it, all in half pennies, without their interfering with my eating. Otherwise I could not have owned a single penny the cursed blind man would not have come upon, for there was not a seam or patch that he did not examine with frequency.

So, as I say, every night I put the key in my mouth and

went to sleep without suspecting that that wizard of a
master of mine would discover it; but when misfortune is
ordained, forethought cannot help. My ill fate, or rather
my sins, so willed it that one night I was sleeping with
the key in my mouth, which must have been open, in
such a position and manner that my breath as I slept
came through the shank of the key, which was in the
shape of a tube, making a loud whistle. This was my
undoing, for my fearful master heard it and thought it
must be the whistle of the snake, and it must certainly
have seemed so.

He got up very quietly with club in hand, and feeling
his way and guided by the sound of the supposed snake,
he came up beside me very quietly so it would not hear
him. And then he got the thought it must be in the straw
where I lay, seeking my warmth. Raising the club high,
thinking that he had found it and could fetch it such a
blow that he would kill it, he gave me such a whack on
the head that he left me senseless and with my pate split
open.

When he realized that he had hit me from the moaning I must have made with the fierce blow, he said that
he bent over me and calling me with loud cries, tried to
arouse me. But when he touched me with his hands and
felt the blood that was flowing from me, he realized the
harm he had done me. He quickly went for a light, and
when he came with it he found me moaning, and still
with the key, which I had not let go, in my mouth, half-in
and half-out, as it must have been when I was whistling
through it.

Wondering what that key could be, the snake-killer pulled it out of my mouth, and saw what it was, because its pattern in no wise differed from his. Then he tried it out, and in this way proved the method of my trick.

The heartless hunter must have said:

"Now I have discovered the mouse and the snake that gave me so much trouble and ate my property."

To what happened in the next three days I can bear no witness, for I spent them in the belly of the whale;[17] but what I have related I heard, when I had come to my senses, from the lips of my master who told it in detail to all who came there.

After three days I came to my senses, and found myself lying in the straw, my head all bandaged and covered with salves and ointments, and asked, in my fright:

"What has happened?"

And the cruel priest replied:

"Verily, verily, I have hunted down the mice and snakes that were ruining me."

And looking about me and finding the state I was in, I quickly suspected my ill fortune.

About this time the neighbors came in with an old woman who was a healer. They began to take the cloths off my head and dress the club wound. And as I had regained my senses, they were greatly pleased and said:

"Now that he has recovered consciousness, God will be pleased to restore his health."

And once more they began to talk over my mishaps,

---

[17] *Like Jonah the prophet, who was in the belly of the whale for three days.*

and laugh at them, while I, poor sinner, wept over them.
Nevertheless, they gave me food, for I was weak with
hunger, and they had trouble bringing me around. Little
by little, after fifteen days, I was able to get up and was
out of danger (though not out of hunger), and half well.

The very next day after I got up, my master took me
by the hand, opened the door, and putting me out in
the street, said to me:

"Lázaro, from today on you are yours and not mine.
Find yourself a master, and go with God. I do not want
such a diligent servant. Beyond the shadow of a doubt,
you have served a blind man."

And making the sign of the cross against me, as
though I were possessed of the devil, he went into his
house and closed the door.

CHAPTER THREE

OF HOW LÁZARO TOOK SERVICE
WITH A SQUIRE AND OF
WHAT ENSUED

And so I was obliged to summon strength from weakness, and little by little, thanks to the help of kindly people, I made my way to this illustrious city of Toledo where, by God's mercy, within a fortnight my wound healed. While I was ailing, someone always gave me alms; but when I was recovered, all I heard was:

"Scamp! Sponger! Go find yourself a good master to serve."

"And where am I to find him," I said to myself, "unless God were to create one, as he did the world?"

Wandering about from door to door with such thoughts and with extremely meager results, for charity had taken wings and ascended to heaven, God so brought it about that I met with a squire who was walking down the street, fittingly dressed, well groomed, seemly in bearing and gesture. He looked at me, and I at him, and he said to me:

"Boy, are you seeking a master?"

I said to him:

"Yes, sir."

"Then follow me," he answered, "for God has done you a service by having you meet with me. You have said some good prayer today."

So I followed him, giving thanks to God for what I
had heard him say and also because it seemed to me, from
his attire and bearing, that he was the person I was looking for.

It was in the morning when I encountered this my
third master. He led me after him through much of the
city. We walked through the market places where bread
and other provisions were sold. I thought, and even
hoped, that he wanted to load me up with what was on
sale, because this was the hour of day when it is customary to buy such supplies; but with rapid strides he
went past these things.

"Perhaps he doesn't find things here to his liking," I
said to myself, "and he wants us to buy them somewhere
else."

We walked about in this fashion until it struck eleven.
Then he went into the cathedral, and I after him, and I
watched him hear Mass and the other divine services
very devoutly, until all was concluded and the people
had left. Then we came out of the church.

At a good pace we started down one of the streets.
Nobody could have been happier than I as I noticed that
we did not bother to buy anything to eat. Said I to myself,
my new master must be the kind of man who buys things
in quantity and the meal is probably ready and of the
sort I long for and really need.

The clock was striking one when we reached a house
before which my master halted, and I with him; and
throwing back the left side of his cape, he pulled a key
out of his sleeve, opened the door, and we went into the

house. The vestibule was so dark and gloomy that it seemed designed to frighten those who entered it; beyond it there was a small patio and good-sized rooms.

When we had entered, he took off his cape, and asking me if my hands were clean, we shook it out and folded it; and carefully blowing the dust off a stone bench, he laid the cape on it. Having done this, he sat down beside it, and asked me at length where I was from and how I had happened to come to that city.

I gave him a longer account than I would have wished, for the hour seemed to me more fitting for him to order me to set the table and serve the soup than for what he was asking of me. Nevertheless, I satisfied him about myself to the best of my ability to lie, telling him my assets, and keeping silent about the rest, for it seemed to me best not to talk too freely. This concluded, he sat on for a time and this seemed to me a bad omen, for it was now almost two o'clock, and I saw he showed no more desire to eat than if he were dead.

As we sat on, I kept turning over in my mind the matter of the locked door and my not hearing the footsteps of a living soul in the house, upstairs or down. All I had seen were bare walls, without chairs, stool, bench, table, or even a chest such as the one I was already acquainted with. In a word, it seemed an enchanted house. At this point he said to me:

"Boy, have you eaten?"

"No, sir," I said, "for it was not yet eight when I encountered Your Worship."

"Well, even though it was so early, I had already eaten,

and I should tell you that when I eat something this way I take nothing more until evening. So you get along as best you can, and later we shall dine."

Your Excellency may well believe that when I heard him say this I was on the point of swooning, not so much from hunger as because I saw clearly how contrary my fortune was. Once more I had a vision of my trials, and wept anew at my sufferings. Once more there came to my mind the reflections I had made to myself when I thought of leaving the priest: mean and miserly though he was, I might encounter another who was worse. In a word, I wept for the hard life I had undergone and my fast approaching death.

Nevertheless, feigning as best I could, I said:

"Sir, I am young, and eating does not concern me too much, thank God. I can boast that among all my companions, I am the most moderate eater, and for this I have been praised by all the masters I have had to this day."

"That is a virtue," said he, "and I shall esteem you the more for it, because gorging is for pigs, and eating temperately for decent men."

"How well I have understood you," I said to myself. "To the devil with all the medicine and virtues these successive masters of mine find in hunger!"

I seated myself to one side of the entrance, and pulled out of my bosom some pieces of bread left from the alms I had received. When he saw what I was doing he said to me:

"Come here, boy. What are you eating?"

I went over to him and showed him the bread. He took the best and biggest of the three pieces there were and said:

"By my faith, this looks like good bread."

"And how good it is! Do you find it so, sir?"

"Indeed, indeed. And where did you come by it? I wonder if it has been kneaded by clean hands?"

"That I cannot say," I answered; "but I do not find the taste of it displeasing."

"So be it," said my poor master, and carrying it to his mouth he began to take as ravenous bites of his piece as I of mine.

"Delicious bread it is, in truth," he said.

And as I realized how the land lay, I made haste, for I saw plainly that if he finished his before I did, he would offer to help me with what was left. And so we finished up almost at the same time. My master brushed off a few very fine crumbs that had dropped on his breast, and going into a small room brought out a chipped and not very new jug; and after drinking, he offered it to me. I, feigning moderation, said:

"Sir, I don't drink wine."

"It's water," he answered, "you can drink it."

Then I took the jug and drank. But not much, for thirst was not my trouble.

So we remained until nightfall, talking of things about which he questioned me and to which I replied as best I knew how. During this time he took me into the chamber where the jug of water we had drunk from stood, and said to me:

"Boy, you stand there and watch how we make up this bed, so you will know how to do it from now on."

I stood at one end and he at the other, and we made up the wretched bed. There was not much making to be done to it, for it consisted of a wicker framework on top of two benches. Over this were spread the bed-clothes, on top of a filthy mattress which, not being accustomed to frequent washings, did not seem a mattress (though it served as such), for it contained far less wool than it would have needed. We smoothed it and did what we could to soften it. This was impossible, for it is difficult to make a hard thing soft. Devil a thing did that sorry saddle-pad have inside it! When it was laid on the framework every single reed showed through, and it looked like the backbone of a skinny hog. And over that gaunt mattress there was a blanket, equally thin, whose color I could not make out.

When the bed was made and it had grown dark, he said to me: "Lázaro, it has grown late, and it's a long way from here to the market. Besides, this city abounds in thieves, and by night they snatch capes. Let's get through the night as best we can, and tomorrow, with the new day, God will show His bounty. For, as I am alone, I have no supplies; these days I have been eating out. But from now on we shall arrange matters differently."

"Sir," I said to him, "let Your Worship have no concern about me, for I know how to spend a night, and more if necessary, without eating."

"You will live longer, and your health will be better," he answered, "because as we were saying, there is nothing in the world so conducive to longevity as eating little."

"If that's the case," said I to myself, "I am never going to die, for I have always observed that rule out of necessity, and I fancy, with my bad luck, I'll keep it all my life."

My master laid himself on the bed, using his breeches and doublet as a pillow, and ordered me to lie down at his feet, which I did. But devil a wink did I sleep, for the reeds and my protruding bones never stopped warring and contending the live-long night. With the hardships, suffering, and hunger I had undergone, I doubt that there was a pound of flesh on my body; moreover, as I had eaten almost nothing that day, I was beside myself with hunger, which is a poor bed-fellow. I cursed myself a thousand times (God forgive me for it!) and my ill-fortune most of the night, and, to make things worse, I was afraid to move for fear of waking him. I implored God a thousand times to let me die.

When morning came we got up and he began to brush and shake out his breeches, doublet, jacket and cape while I went through the farce of helping him! And he took his own sweet time in dressing. I poured water into a basin, he combed his hair, buckled his sword on his belt, and as he was doing so he said to me:

"Boy, if you only knew what a jewel this piece is! Not a gold mark in the world that I would sell it for. No, sir! Not one of all those made by Antonio[18] has edges as keen as this one."

---

[18] *A famous sword-maker of Toledo, which was world-renowned for the quality of its swords.*

And he drew it from the sheath and tested it with his finger, saying:

"You see that? I'll bet I could cut through fleece with it."

Said I to myself: "And I a four pound loaf with my teeth, even though they are not of steel."

He put it back, girded it on, and hung a string of thick beads from his sword belt. And with leisurely pace and erect carriage, gracefully moving body and head, tossing one corner of his cape over his shoulder, and sometimes under his arm, his right hand at his waist, he walked out of the door, saying:

"Lázaro, mind the house while I go to hear Mass, and make the bed, and fetch a jug of water from the river, which is down that way, and lock the door with the key so nobody will steal anything, and put it here by the hinge so I can get in if I return before you get back."

And up the street he went with such a gallant appearance and bearing that a person who did not know him would think him a close relative of the Count of Arcos, or, at least, his gentleman-in-waiting.

"Praised be the Lord," I mused as I saw him depart, "who sends the disease and the cure! Who, seeing this master of mine, would not think, to judge by his air of content, that he had dined well last night, slept in a good bed, and, for all it is so early, eaten a hearty breakfast? How secret are Thy works, Oh Lord, which the people know not! Who would not be deceived by that goodly presence and respectable cape and coat? And who would think that that fine gentleman spent all day yesterday without eating anything but that crust of bread which his servant Lázaro carried around for a day and a night hidden in his bosom where it did not take on much cleanliness, and that today, when he washed his hands and face, for lack of a towel, he had to use his shirttail? Certainly nobody would suspect it. Oh Lord, how many of that kind must thou have scattered about the world, who suffer for the sake of their faded honor what they would not suffer for Thee!"

Meditating and considering these and many other things, I stood at the door until my master had disappeared down the long and narrow street. When he was out of sight I went back in the house and in the twinkling of an eye I went over it from top to bottom without let or hindrance, for there was nothing to stop me. I made up the hard black bed, took the jug and made my way to the river, where in a garden I saw my master in lively conversation with two veiled women of the kind that apparently are never wanting in that place. Many of them are in the habit of setting out on a summer morning for those cool banks to refresh themselves and to have lunch without carrying the wherewithal, trusting that someone will turn up who will provide it, the gentlemen of the city having so accustomed them.

As I was saying, he was with them, playing the rôle of an impassioned lover, saying more sweet nothings than Ovid[19] ever wrote. And when they saw him amorously

---

[19] *Publius Ovidius Naso, 43 B.C.-18 A.D. Roman poet, famous for his love poetry.*

inclined, they had no hesitation in asking him to give
them lunch, for which they would make the customary
payment.

But he, as chill of purse as warm of heart, was seized
by such a cramp that his face went pale and he began
to stammer and make feeble excuses.

They, who must have been experienced, as soon as
they observed the symptoms of his illness, left him for
what he was.

I, who was munching some cabbage stalks on which
I breakfasted, hurried back to the house dutifully, as
became a new servant, without being seen by my master.
I intended to sweep part of it, for it stood badly in need
of such attention, but I could find nothing for the purpose. I turned over in my mind what I should do, and
decided to wait for my master until midday to see if perchance he would return with something for us to eat;
but my vigil was in vain.

When I saw that it was two o'clock and he had not
come, and hunger was ravaging me, I locked the door,
put the key where he had ordered, and went back to
my old trade. In a low, plaintive voice, my hands crossed
on my breast, and with God before my eyes and His name
on my tongue, I began to beg bread beside the gateways
and at the houses I judged best. And as I had acquired
this trade almost with my mother's milk, that is to say, I
had learned it with that great master, the blind man, I
proved such an apt pupil that although this city is not
known for its charity, and it had not been a prosperous
year, so well did I ply my trade that before the clock

struck four, I already had as many pounds of bread safely stored away in my stomach, and some two more in my sleeves and shirt front. On my way back to my lodging I passed a tripe shop, and begged alms of one of the women there, and she gave me a piece of cow's foot and some scraps of boiled tripe.

My fine master was already there when I reached the house, his cape folded and laid on the bench, and he was walking up and down the patio. As I entered he came toward me. I thought he was going to scold me for being late; but God ordered things differently.

He inquired where I had been, and I said to him:

"Sir, I was here until it struck two, and when I saw that Your Worship had not come back, I went about the city to commend myself to the good people and they gave me this which you see."

I showed him the bread and the tripe, which I was carrying in a corner of my shirttail, at the sight of which his face lighted up and he said:

"Well, I had been waiting for you to eat, and when I saw that you were not coming, I ate. But you have behaved like a decent person in what you have done, for it is better to beg in the name of God than to steal. And as I hope for His favor, what you have done seems well to me. I enjoin upon you only not to let it be known that you live with me, for the sake of my honor, though I fully believe it must be a secret, so little known am I in this city. Would that I had never come to it."

"Lose all fear on that score, sir," I said to him, "for devil a person needs to ask me such a thing, or I to tell it."

"Well then, eat, poor wretch. And if it please God, we shall soon be free of want, although I tell you that ever since I set foot in this house nothing has gone well with me. It must be on ill-boded soil. For there are unlucky, bad-omened houses which cast their evil fortune on those who live in them. Undoubtedly this is one of them; but I promise that when the month is up I shall not stay on here, even if they were to give it to me."

I sat down on the edge of the bench and so he would not think me a glutton I said nothing about what I had already eaten. And I began to bite and munch on my tripe and bread, watching out of the corner of my eye my unhappy master, who did not take his eyes off my shirt-tail, which I was using as a plate. May God take as much pity on me as I on him, for I felt what he was feeling, as I had suffered the same thing many times, and suffered it every day. I wondered if it would be fitting for me to offer him some; but, as he had told me that he had eaten, I was afraid he would not accept my invitation. In a word, I was wishing the poor wretch would join me, and break his fast as he had done the previous day, for the occasion was better as the food was more abundant and my hunger less.

God was pleased to satisfy my desire and, as I think, his, too. Because when I began to eat and he went walking up and down, he came over beside me and said:

"I must say, Lázaro, that you have a grace in your way of eating such as I have never in my life seen in anyone else, and nobody can watch you without getting an appetite, even if he doesn't have one."

"The keen appetite you have," I said to myself, "makes mine seem beautiful to you."

With all, it seemed to me I should give him a helping hand, for he was doing all he could, and opening the way for me. So I said to him:

"Sir, good tools make a good workman. This bread is delicious, and this cow's foot is so well cooked and seasoned that it would tempt anyone."

"Cow's foot, did you say?"

"Yes, sir."

"Let me tell you that is the best eating in the world, and I wouldn't trade you pheasant for it."

"Well, taste it, sir, and you will see how good it is."

I put the cow's paw into his, and three or four pieces of the whitest bread. He sat down beside me and began to eat, like one who was famished, polishing off every one of the little bones better than a hound could have done.

"With garlic sauce," he said, "this is a very tasty dish."

"It's a better sauce you are eating it with—hunger," said I under my breath.

"Good Heavens, it tasted to me as though I hadn't eaten a morsel all day."

"May I have as many good years as that is true," I thought to myself.

He asked for the jug of water, and I gave it to him just as I had fetched it from the river. As no water had been taken from it, it was a sign that my master had had nothing to eat. We drank, and in good content went to bed as the night before.

To avoid becoming repetitious, I may say that we spent some eight or ten days in this fashion, the poor sinner setting out in the morning with that air of well-being and gravity to fill his stomach with air, while poor Lázaro was the dupe that brought him bread.

Many a time I pondered on my evil star and how, fleeing from the miserly masters I had served, and seeking to better myself, I had encountered one who not only did not feed me, but whom I had to feed. Yet withal, I liked him well, for I saw that he had nothing and could not do otherwise. I felt pity for him rather than ill will. And many times to be able to bring him something, I went without it myself.

One morning the poor devil got out of bed in his shirt and went upstairs to relieve himself, and while he was gone, to settle my doubts, I unfolded his jacket and breeches, which he had left at the head of the bed, and found a velvet purse, creased into a hundred folds, and without a penny, or a sign that it had held one for a long time.

"This fellow," said I, "is poor and nobody can give what he does not have; but the miserly blind man and the mean skinflint of a priest, both of whom received in the name of God, the one from his hand-kissing faithful, the other thanks to his glib tongue, starved me to death, so it is just to dislike them and have pity on this one."

As God is my witness, even today when I encounter one of his type with that same haughty bearing, I feel pity for him, wondering if he suffers what I saw that one undergo. For all his poverty I was happier to serve him than the others, for the reasons I have stated. There was only one thing about him that displeased me a little. I should have wished he were somewhat less presumptuous, and that his vanity would diminish as his need increased. But, as far as I can make out, it is the customary code observed by them: even if they haven't a penny to their names, they must keep up appearances. May the Lord help them, for they will carry this affliction to the grave.

Finding myself in this state, undergoing the trials I have told, my ill fortune (which never wearied of pursuing me) so disposed it that this difficult and shameful existence should not endure. It so happened that as it had been a bad year in those parts, the city council decreed that all indigent non-residents should leave the city, and it was proclaimed by the town crier that those found there after the allotted time would suffer the lash. Thus, when the law went into effect four days after it had been proclaimed, I saw a procession of beggars being whipped through the main streets. This so frightened me that from then on I never ventured to beg.

With this, whoever has the imagination for it can see the penury of my home and the sadness and silence of its dwellers, which was such that at times two or three days went by without our eating a morsel or saying a word. My life was saved by some kindly women, cotton-spinners, who made bonnets and lived next door to us, with whom I had a neighborly acquaintance. From the pittance they received, they gave me some trifle with which I assuaged my pangs of hunger a little.

And I did not feel as sorry for myself as for my sorry

master, who did not taste a mouthful of food in a week.
At any rate, during all that time we did not eat in the
house. I do not know how or where he went or what he
ate. And to see him coming down the street at midday,
straight as a ramrod, leaner than a thoroughbred hound!
And out of deference to his touchy honor, he would take
a straw, and even of those there were not too many in
the house, and go out picking his teeth, which had nothing between them, still complaining about the ill-omened
house, saying:

"It is plain that this house brings bad luck. As you
can see, it is gloomy, sad, dark. As long as we are in it,
things will go badly with us. I cannot wait for the month
to be up so we can leave."

Now, while we were in this piteous and hungry state,
one day, I do not know by what stroke of luck, a *real*
came into the hands of my master. With it he came home
as proud as if he possessed the treasures of Venice, and
with a carefree, happy gesture he handed it to me, saying:

"Take this, Lázaro, for God is opening His hand. Go
to the market and buy bread and wine and meat; we're
going to splurge! And I want you to know for your satis-
faction that I have rented another house, and we're not
going to stay in this one after the month is up. A pox on
it and whoever laid its first tile, for nothing has gone
right since I set foot in it. By our Lord, as long as I have
been living in it, not a drop of wine nor a bite of meat
have I taken, nor have I known rest, with the sight of
it and its gloom and sadness. But go and come back
quickly, for today we shall eat like royalty."

I took my *real* and jug, and setting wings to my feet, started up the street toward the market, full of cheer and happiness. But, to what avail, if it is written in my stars that no pleasure shall come to me without alarm? And so it was with this. While hurrying up the street, going over in my mind how I would use the money to the best advantage, and giving infinite thanks to God, who had willed that my master receive it, in an evil hour I encountered a corpse which was being carried down the street on a litter by many friars and a crowd of people.

I flattened myself against the wall to give them room, and as the body passed, one who must have been the wife of the dead man was following the bier, dressed in mourning, and accompanied by many other women; she was weeping aloud and saying:

"My lord and husband, where are they taking you? To that sad and cheerless abode, to that dark and gloomy abode, to the abode where none eat or drink."

When I heard that it was as though the sky had fallen on me, and I said:

"Oh, God have mercy on me. They are taking this dead man to my house."

I turned back, and making my way through the people ran back down the street as fast as my legs would carry me to my house. When I got there I slammed the door shut, calling on my master for aid and protection, throwing my arms around him, to come and help me keep them from entering. Somewhat provoked, not knowing what had happened, he said:

"What is the meaning of this, boy? What are you

shouting about? What ails you? Why have you closed the door with such fury?"

"Oh, sir," I answered, "come quickly, for they are bringing us a dead man!"

"What are you saying?" he answered.

"I came upon him down the street, and his wife was saying: 'My lord and husband, where are they taking you? To that sad and cheerless house, to that dark and gloomy house, to the house where none eat or drink!' Sir, they are bringing him here."

When my master heard this, although there was no reason for mirth, he laughed so much that for a long time he was unable to talk. During this time I had fastened the bar of the door, and had my shoulder against it the better to hold it. The people went past with the corpse, and I still had misgivings lest they bring him into our house. And after my good master was more surfeited with laughing than with eating, he said to me:

"Truly, Lázaro, from the lamentations of the widow you were right in what you thought; but inasmuch as God has ordered it better and they are going by, open the door; open the door and go for food."

"Wait, master, wait until they have gone from the street."

Finally my master went to the street door and opened it, giving me courage which I needed after the fright and dismay I had undergone, and I set forth again. But although we ate well that day, devil the pleasure I took in it. For three days I did not get back my color. And my master laughed heartily every time he recalled my words.

In this fashion I continued with my third and poor master, this squire, for a number of days, and all the time I was curious to know the reason for his coming to this part of the country and remaining there. For, from the first day I entered his service I realized he was not from this city, because of the little acquaintance and few dealings he had with the natives of it.

Finally my desire was fulfilled and I came to know what had puzzled me. For one day when we had eaten reasonably well and he was fairly happy, he told me his affairs, and said he was from Old Castile and had left his province solely because he would not remove his hat to a neighboring knight.

"Sir," said I, "if he was what you say, and outranked you, were you not at fault in not removing yours first, since you say that he took his off to you?"

"He is what I say, and he does outrank me, and it is also true that he took his off to me; but inasmuch as I always took mine off first, it would have been fitting for him to have done so first some time."

"Sir, it seems to me that I would not have taken that into consideration, particularly with my superiors who are wealthier than I."

"You are but a boy," he replied, "and you don't understand these matters of honor, which today represents the sole treasure of well-born men. For I would have you know that I am, as you see, a squire; but, as God is my witness, if I meet a count in the street, and he doesn't completely and properly remove his cap to me, the next time I encounter him I will make it a point to go into a house, pretending that I have some business there, or cross over to the other side of the street, if there is one, before he reaches me, so as not to remove mine to him. For an hidalgo owes nothing save to God and king; nor is it right that being well-born, he should fail by one iota to hold himself in high regard. I recall that one day in my province I had words with an officer and almost struck him, because every time I met him he said to me: 'God keep Your Worship.'

"Have you no manners, you low-born scoundrel, that you say to me 'God keep you,' as though I were just anybody? From then on, he took off his cap and greeted me as he should."

"And isn't that the right way for one man to greet another?" I said. "To say to him 'God keep you?' "

"How ignorant you are," he said. "That is the way you speak to those of low degree; but to the well-born, like myself, you must say at least: 'I kiss Your Worship's hands,' or, at least, 'Sir, I kiss your hands,' if the one who is speaking is a knight. And from that neighbor of mine, with whose greeting I was fed up, I would no longer suffer, nor will I suffer from any man in the world, except the king, that he say to me 'God keep you.' "

"Sinner that I am," said I, "for that reason He gives so little thought to keeping you, for you will not let anyone ask it of Him."

"Besides," he said, "I am not so poor that I do not have in my province, sixteen leagues from where I was born on that sloping street of Valladolid, houses and lands, which if they were repaired and well-cultivated, would be worth better than two hundred times a thousand *maravedís,* so fine and good they might be made. And I have a dovecot which, if it were not broken down, as it is, would provide each year more than two hundred squabs. And other things, which I do not care to mention, I left because of this offense to my honor. And I came to this city, thinking to find here a good situation; but it has not turned out as I thought. Canons and churchmen I find in abundance; but they are so limited in their outlook that nothing can change their ways. Middle-rank knights have solicited me, too; but to serve them is unpleasant, because you have to play second fiddle to them, and if you are not so inclined, 'Go with God,' they tell you. And most of the time payments are few and far between, and more often than not, you work for your keep.

"When their conscience pricks them, and they want to remunerate your labors, they pay you off in a sweat-stained doublet or a frayed cape or coat. Even when one takes service with a man of title, he still undergoes privations. Tell me, have I not, perchance, the requisites to serve and satisfy such as they? By Heaven, if I should come upon such a one I think I could be an excellent privy counselor to him, and do him a thousand services, for I would know how to lie to him as well as the next one, and leave him well pleased. I would laugh heartily at his quips and mannerisms, though these were not the best in the world. I would never say a thing to annoy him, however much it might be to his advantage. I'd be zealous of his person in word and deed. Nor would I kill myself doing well things that would not meet his eye.

And, when he was around to hear, I'd remonstrate with the servants so it would seem that I was solicitous of everything that concerned him. If he quarreled with one of his servitors, I'd put in a sly word to kindle his wrath and yet seem to be taking the part of the culprit. I'd speak well of what pleased him, and, on the contrary, be malicious, mocking, and a trouble-maker among those of the house and outsiders; I'd search and find out other people's affairs to bring him this gossip, and many other accomplishments of this sort which are the vogue in palaces today and please their masters well.

"For they have no desire for virtuous men around them; rather they despise and scorn them, and call them fools, and persons with no capacity for dealings, or unworthy of the master's trust. And with these masters the cunning today employ the arts that I would use, but my ill fortune does not let me find one."

In these words my master, too, bemoaned his adverse fortune, giving me an account of his gifted person.

Now, as we were thus discoursing, there appeared at the door a man and an old woman. The man asked him for the rent of the house, and the old woman, for that of the bed. They added up the account, and for two months it came to what he would not come by in a year. I think it amounted to twelve or thirteen *reales*. He answered them courteously, saying that he would go to the market and change a doubloon, and that they should come back in the afternoon; but his departure was without return.

They came back in the afternoon, but it was too late. I told them that he had not yet returned. Night came, but not my master; I was afraid to stay in the house alone, and I went to the neighbor women, told them what had happened, and slept there.

When morning came the creditors returned, and asked for my master, but at this other door. The women answered them:

"Here is his boy and the key to the door."

They asked me about him and I told them I did not know where he was, that he had not returned since he went out to change the doubloon and that, in my opinion, he had taken leave of them and me with the change.

When they heard this they went for a constable and a notary. And, lo, they came back with them and took the key and called me and witnesses and opened the door and went in to attach the property of my master to satisfy their debt. They went over the whole house and found it as bare as I have related, and they said to me:

"What has become of the belongings of your master, his chests and wall hangings and fine housewares?"

"I know nothing about that," I answered them.

"Without doubt," they said, "last night they made off with them and hid them somewhere. Constable, arrest this boy, for he knows where they are."

The constable took me by the collar, saying:

"Boy, you are under arrest unless you reveal the whereabouts of your master's belongings."

I had never found myself in such a predicament before (I had been laid hold of by the collar many a time, but lightly, to lead the blind man) and I was greatly frightened. In tears, I promised to answer all their questions.

"Very well," they said. "Now tell everything you know and don't be afraid."

The notary sat down on a bench to write out the inventory, asking me what he possessed.

"Gentlemen," I said, "what my master owned, so he told me, was a fine lot of houses and a tumbledown dovecot."

"Very good," they answered. "However little that is worth, it will be enough to satisfy the debt. And in what part of the city does he have them?" they inquired.

"In his province," I answered.

"God help us, here is a fine business," they said. "And where is his province?"

"He told me he was from Old Castile," I answered.

The constable and the notary laughed heartily, saying:

"There is the proof you need to collect your debt, even if it were larger."

The neighbor women, who were standing by, said:

"Gentlemen, this is an innocent child, and he has been with this squire only a few days, and he knows no more about him than Your Worships do; the little sinner used to come to our house and we'd give him what we could to eat for charity's sake, and at night he went to sleep with him."

In view of my innocence, they unhanded me, and let me go free. And the constable and the notary asked the man and woman for their fees. This gave rise to a great dispute and outcry, for they claimed that they were under no obligation to pay as there was nothing to attach. The others claimed that because of attending to this they had lost other business of more profit.

In the end, after much hullabaloo, the constable's assistant picked up the old woman's mattress, whose weight he hardly felt, and the five of them went off arguing. I don't know how it ended. I think the scurvy mattress must have paid for everything. And it served it right, for when it should have been reposing and resting from its labors, it was hiring itself out.

Thus, as I have related, my poor third master left me, which was final proof of my ill fortune. For, using me as spitefully as it could, it ordered my affairs so much in reverse that while masters are usually left by their servants, this one was not so dealt with by me, but rather it was my master who left me and ran away.

CHAPTER FOUR

HOW LÁZARO TOOK SERVICE
WITH A MERCEDERIAN FRIAR
AND WHAT HAPPENED WITH HIM

I had to look for a fourth, and this was a Mercederian friar to whom the women I mentioned took me; they called him a kinsman. He was not fond of singing in the choir or of taking his meals in the monastery, but was mad about roaming abroad, and greatly given to lay matters and visiting; so much so that I think he wore out more shoes than the rest of the convent put together. He gave me the first shoes I ever wore in my life, but they lasted less than a week. Nor would I have lasted longer at the pace he kept, so for this and other reasons which I shall not mention I left him.

CHAPTER FIVE

HOW LÁZARO TOOK SERVICE
WITH A PARDONER AND
OF THE THINGS THAT OCCURRED
WITH HIM

The fifth it was my lot to encounter was a pardoner, the most brazen, shameless, and wholesale seller of indulgences that I ever saw or hope to see, or anyone ever saw, so I believe. He had methods and techniques, and kept inventing very subtle devices.

When he came to a village where the papal bull was to be presented, the first thing he did was to make certain little gifts of slight importance to the clergy or priests: a head of Murcian lettuce, a couple of sweet limes or oranges in season, a peach or two, a russet pear apiece. Thus he put them in a receptive mood to favor his enterprise and call their parishioners to acquire the indulgences.

By the way they thanked him, he gauged their ability. If they said that they understood Latin, he did not proffer a word in that tongue lest he commit an error, but employed a clear, fine-sounding vernacular with great eloquence. And if he saw that the clergymen in question were of the type that are ordained by paying money rather than by studying for holy orders, he passed himself off among them as a Saint Thomas Aquinas, and talked for two hours on end in Latin. At least that was what it seemed, though it was not.

When the indulgences were not accepted willingly, he employed sterner measures. At times he threatened, and at others he had recourse to the most wily methods. And as to relate all those I saw him use would take too long, I shall tell of one that was very subtle and ingenious, which will evidence his ability.

In a village of La Sagra in Toledo he had been preaching for two or three days, employing his customary tactics, and they had not bought an indulgence from him nor, as far as I could see, did they have any intention of doing so. He was in a fury at this, and turning over in his mind what measures he should take, he decided to summon the village and promulgate the bull the next morning.

That night, after dinner, he and the constable began to gamble to see who should pay for the dessert. They began to quarrel over the game and to have words. He called the constable a thief, and the other called him a cheat. Whereupon my master, the pardoner, picked up a lance that was in the hall where they were gaming. The constable reached for the sword at his belt.

With the uproar and shouts we all began to make, the lodgers and neighbors came up and intervened. The two of them, greatly angered, tried to get free from those between them, in order to kill each other. But as the number of people grew with the noise, and the house was full of them, seeing that they could not attack one another with arms, they hurled insulting words. Among other things the constable said my master was a cheat and that the bulls he promulgated were false.

Finally, when the people of the village saw that they were unable to make peace between them, they decided to take the constable away from the inn to another place, and this made my master very angry. After the lodgers and neighbors had implored him to lay aside his wrath and go to bed, he went, and thus we all got some sleep.

The next morning my master went to the church and ordered the bell rung for Mass and for the sermon in which the bull would be promulgated. The people gathered, muttering against the indulgences, saying they were spurious and that the constable himself had revealed this when the two were quarrelling. So that, while they were reluctant to accept the bull before, now, with what had happened, they were completely against it.

The pardoner arose in the pulpit, and began to preach and urge the people not to forego the benefits and indulgence the holy bull conferred. When he was at the peak of his sermon, into the church came the constable, and after saying a prayer, he got to his feet and in a loud, measured voice, began to speak:

"Good people, hearken to a word from me, and afterwards you can listen to whomever you like. I came here with this impostor who is preaching to you. He tricked me and said that if I helped him in this business we would divide the profits. And now that I see the harm this would do to my conscience and your pockets, repentant of what I did, I openly declare to you that the bulls he is promulgating are false, and that you should not believe him nor acquire them, that I have no part in them, direct or indirect, and that from this moment I am laying aside my wand of office, which I now throw on the floor. If at any time this man should be punished for his deceit, you are witnesses to the fact that I have nothing to do with him, nor do I help him; on the contrary, I am opening your eyes and proclaiming his wickedness."

With this he concluded his declaration. Some God-fearing men who were among the congregation were ready to arise and throw the constable out of the church to avoid a scandal. But my master restrained them, and ordered them all, under pain of excommunication, not to hinder him but to let him say all he wished. Thus he, too, remained silent while the constable said all that I have related.

When he had finished, my master said that if he had anything more to say, he should say it.

The constable answered:

"There is much more to be said about you and your trickery; but for the time being let this suffice."

The pardoner knelt in the pulpit, and clasping his hands and looking heavenward, he said:

"Lord God, from whom nothing is hidden and all is manifest, and to whom nothing is impossible, rather everything is possible: Thou knowest the truth, and how unjustly I have been reviled. As far as I am concerned, I forgive him, that Thou, O Lord, mayest forgive me. Pay no heed to one who does not know what he is doing or saying; but I implore and beg Thee for the sake of justice not to overlook the affront done Thee. Perchance someone present, who may have thought of taking this blessed indulgence, because of giving credence to the false words of that man, will refrain from doing so. And inasmuch as harm to a fellow man is so great, I beg Thee, Lord, not to let it go unpunished; perform a miracle here and now, and let it be after this fashion: if what that man says is true, that I am the purveyor of evil and false-hood, let this pulpit be shattered with me in it, and fall seven fathoms underground where neither it nor I shall ever be seen again; but if what I say is true, and that man, led astray by the devil to deprive those here of this great good, is lying, let him be punished and his wicked-ness made known to all."

My devout master had no more than finished his prayer when the black-hearted constable fell from his seat with such a thud that the whole church echoed, and he began to roar and foam at the mouth, with his face contorted, flinging his hands and feet about, and writh-ing from side to side on the ground.

The uproar and shouts of the people were so great that they could not hear one another. Some of them were terrified and filled with horror.

"God help and protect him," said some. Others: "It serves him right for bearing false witness."

Finally, some of those present, and not without con-siderable fear, it seemed to me, approached him and held down his arms, with which he was dealing out vigorous blows to those near him. Others grabbed him by the legs and pinned them down, because there was never a sly mule that landed more vicious kicks. And they held him like that for a long time. More than fifteen men surrounded him, and he was flailing blows with his hands on all sides, and if they were not careful, struck them in the face.

During all this my master was kneeling in the pulpit, his hands and eyes heavenward, in a divine transport, while the weeping and outcries that filled the church were unable to distract him from his mystic contemplation.

Those good men came over to him and with cries aroused him, begging him to help that unfortunate wretch who was dying, and to bear him no ill will because of what had taken place between them or his evil words, for he had already received his just due; and if in any wise he could help to free the man from the danger and suffering he was undergoing, to do so for the love of God, for they saw clearly how the guilty one had erred, and how truth and goodness were on the pardoner's side, for at his request for vengeance the Lord had not withheld punishment.

The pardoner, like one awakening from a sweet dream, looked at them, and looked at the offender, and at all those standing about, and in slow and measured words said to them:

"Good people, you should never plead for a man on whom God has so manifestly laid his hand; but as He has commanded us never to return evil for evil and to forgive those who spitefully use us, with confidence we can implore Him to carry out what He enjoins upon us;

may His Majesty forgive this one who offended Him by putting obstacles in the way of His holy faith. Let us all pray to Him."

With this he descended from the pulpit and exhorted them to pray to Our Lord with all devotion that He consent to forgive that sinner and restore him to health and his right mind, and cast the devil from him, if His Majesty had allowed the fiend to enter into him because of his great sins.

All of them knelt down, and before the altar with the priests they began to chant a litany in a low voice. My master came with the cross and holy water, and after having chanted over him, with his hands raised toward heaven and his eyes showing only a little of the whites, he began a prayer as long as it was devout, with which he made all the congregation weep, as they are in the habit of doing during the sermons on the Passion, when preacher and congregation are equally devout. He implored Our Lord not to desire the death of that sinner, but his life and repentance, led astray, as he was, by the devil and blinded by death and sin, and to pardon him and give him life and health, that he might repent and confess his sins.

And when he had done this, he ordered the indulgence brought and laid it on his head. Immediately the sinner of a constable began to show signs of recovery and of coming to himself. And once he had recovered his sound judgment, he threw himself at the feet of the pardoner, and begged for forgiveness. He confessed that he had said

what he did at the orders and behest of the devil, in part
to do the pardoner harm and avenge himself for their
quarrel, but principally because the devil suffered greatly
on account of the good that would come from accepting
the bull.

My master forgave him, and friendship between them
was restored. And there was such a rush to take the bull
that hardly a soul in the church but acquired it, husband and wife, sons and daughters, youths and maidens.

The news of what had occurred spread through the
neighboring villages, and by the time he reached them,
no sermon was needed, nor appearance in the church, for
they came to the inn for it as though it were pears that
were being given away free. So in ten or a dozen villages
in those parts that we visited, my master distributed as
many thousand indulgences without preaching a sermon.

When the first performance was put on, I confess that
I, like the others, was terrified by it and thought it was
true; but afterwards when I saw the jests and mocking
that passed between my master and the constable con-
cerning this business, I realized how it had been devised
by the artful cunning of my master.

And though I was only a boy, I found it very amusing,
and I said to myself:

"How many tricks of this sort these impostors must
play on innocent folk."

In conclusion, I stayed with this fifth master of mine
for nearly four months, during which time I suffered also
many trials.

CHAPTER SIX

OF HOW LÁZARO TOOK SERVICE WITH A CHAPLAIN AND WHAT OCCURRED

After this I took service with a tambourine painter, to grind his colors, and with him, too, I suffered a thousand hardships.

As by this time I was a well-grown boy, one day when I went into the cathedral one of the chaplains took me into his employ. And he gave me a donkey, and four water jars and a whip, and I began to sell water in the city. This was the first rung by which I mounted the ladder of good living, because I had enough to eat. Every day I gave my master thirty *maravedís* that I had earned, and could keep anything over that amount. On Saturdays my earnings were for myself.

Things went so well with me in this calling, that at the end of four years during which I followed it, by hoarding my money carefully I saved enough to outfit myself decently in second-hand clothing. I bought a jerkin of old fustian, a worn coat with braided sleeves and collar, a cape that had once been fuzzy, and a sword, one of the early ones made by Cuellar. When I had attired myself decently, I told my master he could take back his donkey, for I no longer wanted to work at that trade.

CHAPTER SEVEN

OF HOW LÁZARO TOOK SERVICE WITH A CONSTABLE AND WHAT HAPPENED TO HIM

When I had taken my leave of the chaplain, I hired myself to a constable as a bailiff. But I stayed with him for a very short time, as it seemed to me a dangerous calling, especially one night when certain fugitives from the law chased me and my master with stones and sticks. And they roughly handled my master, who stayed behind, though they never overtook me. With this I called off our arrangement.

And turning over in my mind how I could hit upon some way to earn my living that would be easy and yield something to provide for my old age, God was pleased to illuminate me and set my feet on a profitable path. And with the help I received from friends and superiors, all the sufferings and trials I had undergone until then were compensated for by my achieving what I sought. This was a government job, for I have seen that none prosper except those who hold such.

With this I live, and continue today in the service of God and Your Excellency. My job consists in acting as crier of the wines on sale in this city, and of auctions, and of things that have been lost, and accompanying those who suffer for justice's sake, setting forth their crimes: in plain language, a town crier.

Things have gone so well with me, and I have made such good use of my office, that nearly everything pertaining thereto goes through my hands. So much so, that in the whole city, if anyone has wine or anything to sell, they know that if Lázaro de Tormes does not handle the matter, they will not receive a profit.

At this season, in view of my success and my good livelihood, the archpriest of Saint Salvador, my master and Your Excellency's servant and friend, having come to know me as I cried his wines, decided to marry me to a servant girl of his. And as I saw that from a person like him only good and profit could come to me, I agreed thereto. Thus I married her, and up to now, I have not repented of it.

For in addition to being a good girl, industrious and obliging, I have in my master, the archpriest, all help and favor. And always during the year he gives her from time to time, a measure of wheat; at holiday time, meat, occasionally a couple of loaves, and his cast-off hose. And he rented a house for us alongside his own, and we eat with him nearly every Sunday and feast day.

Evil tongues, of which there is no lack nor ever will be, never leave us in peace, saying I don't know what (and then again I do) when they see my wife go to make his bed and cook his food. May God be more merciful to them than they are to the truth!

Because in addition to her being a woman who does

not like such jests, my master has promised me something I believe he will carry out. He spoke to me at length one day in front of her, saying:

"Lázaro de Tormes, anyone who hearkens to evil tongues will never prosper. I say this, for it would not surprise me if someone wondered, seeing your wife enter and leave my house. She enters with all honor to herself and to you. This I can promise you. Therefore, pay no attention to what they may say, but to what concerns you—your own advantage, I mean.

"Sir," I said to him, "I made up my mind to seek the company of the good. To be sure, there are those of my friends who have said something about this, and more than three times they have assured me that before she married me she had given birth three times, with all respect to Your Worship and her presence."

Whereupon my wife swore such oaths that I thought the house would sink into the ground and us with it. And then she began to weep, and curse the one who had wed her to me. She was so affected that I wished I had died rather than to have made that remark. But between my master and myself, we so besought and reassured her, that she stopped her weeping on my swearing that never again in all my life would I mention anything of the sort, and that I was pleased and satisfied that she should come and go, by night and by day, being fully persuaded of her virtue. And thus the three of us were well satisfied.

Until this day nobody has heard a word between us

about this matter; on the contrary, when I feel that someone is on the point of saying something about her, I cut him short and say:

"Look, if you are a friend of mine, do not say anything to vex me, for I do not consider him a friend who causes me trouble, above all, if he tries to sow discord between me and my wife. For she is the thing I most prize in this world, and I love her better than myself. And in her God has conferred on me a thousand blessings, and far more than I deserve. For I will swear by the consecrated Host that no better woman lives within the gates of Toledo. And whoever says the contrary will have to answer to me."

In this way they say nothing to me and I have peace in my home.

This was the same year that our victorious emperor[20] entered this noble city of Toledo and held his parliament here, and there was great rejoicing and festivity, as Your Excellency has probably heard.

At long last I was prosperous, and at the zenith of all good fortune.

---

[20] *Charles V. Although the date is not certain, as parliament met in Toledo in 1525 and in 1538, it was probably the former, shortly after the battle of Pavia in Italy, where the Spanish forces defeated the army of the French king, Francis I, and took him prisoner.*

WORLD CLASSICS IN TRANSLATION

New frontiers of reading adventure open up when you explore these expert modern translations of masterpieces of France, Spain, Germany, Spanish America. Language barriers are no longer an obstacle to your full enjoyment of the great literature that you have so long wanted to read. All in attractive editions at modest cost.

BARRON'S EDUCATIONAL SERIES